Collins

Easy Learning
Spelling
Age 5-7

My name is _____.

I am _____ years old.

I go to _____ School.

Karina Law

How to use this book

- Find a quiet, comfortable place to work, away from other distractions.
- Tackle one topic at a time.
- Help with reading the instructions where necessary, and ensure that your child understands what to do.
- Encourage your child to check their own answers as they complete each activity.
- Discuss with your child what they have learnt.
- Let your child return to their favourite pages once they have been completed, to talk about the activities.
- Reward your child with plenty of praise and encouragement.

Special features

Yellow boxes: Introduce a topic and outline the key spelling ideas.

 Suggests when a dictionary may be needed for help with spelling.

Learning a new word

When your child is learning a new word, help them to practise using the 'Look and say, cover, write, check' method.

- Look at the word and say it aloud.
- Cover it.
- Write it.
- Check it.

You could also try the following ideas:

- Break the word up into smaller parts, for example, cup-board.
- Pronounce the word exactly as it is written, for example, Wed-nes-day.
- Break the word up into separate phonemes (sounds), for example, sh-ee-p.

Published by Collins
An imprint of HarperCollins*Publishers*
77–85 Fulham Palace Road
Hammersmith
London
W6 8JB

Browse the complete Collins catalogue at
www.collins.co.uk

First published in 2006
© HarperCollins*Publishers* Limited 2008

10 9 8 7 6

ISBN-13 978-0-00-730096-9

The author asserts the moral right to be
identified as the author of this work.

All rights reserved. No part of this publication
may be reproduced, stored in a retrieval
system, or transmitted in any form or by any
means, electronic, mechanical, photocopying,
recording or otherwise, without the prior
written permission of the Publisher or a
licence permitting restricted copying in the
United Kingdom issued by the Copyright
Licensing Agency Ltd., 90 Tottenham Court
Road, London W1T 4LP.

British Library Cataloguing in Publication Data
A Catalogue record for this publication is
available from the British Library

Written by Karina Law
Design and layout by Graham M Brasnett
Illustrated by Andy Tudor
Cover design by Susi Martin
Cover illustration by John Haslan
Printed and bound by Printing Express,
Hong Kong

Contents

Short vowels

There are five vowels.

a e i o u

Most words in the English language contain at least one vowel.

Q1 Write the missing vowel in each word.

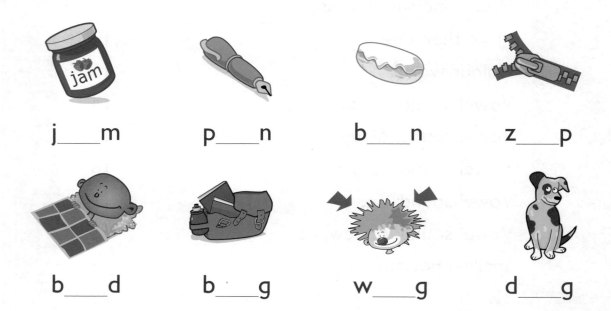

j____m   p____n   b____n   z____p

b____d   b____g   w____g   d____g

Q2 Change the vowel in each word to make a new word.

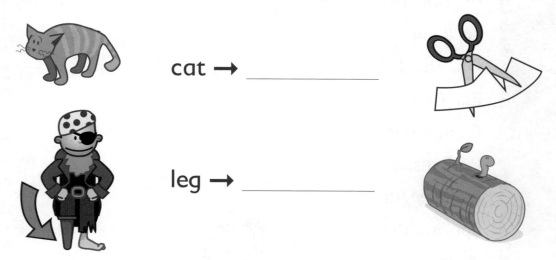

cat → _____

leg → _____

Rhyming words

Rhyming words end with the same sound.

a wet pet

Q1 Circle the picture that rhymes with the word.

bed

box

cap

Q2 Look at the circled words. Find the words that rhyme with them and circle them in the same colour.

hat sun peg bat win beg bin

pot dot

hot rat tin

run leg fun

Long vowels with e

Say the word. Add the letter **e**. Say the new word.
Can you hear a change in the vowel sound?

  cap + e → cape

The vowel in **cap** is a **short vowel**.
When we add **e** to this word, the first vowel becomes a **long vowel**.

Q1 Add **e** to the end of each word to make a new word.

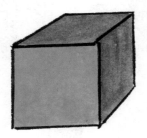

cub → cub____

not → not____

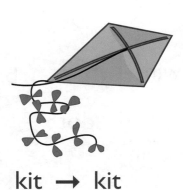

kit → kit____

plan → plan____

Q2 Write words that rhyme.

m
r
sh
+ ake

cake _____

_____   _____

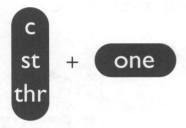
c
st
thr
+ one

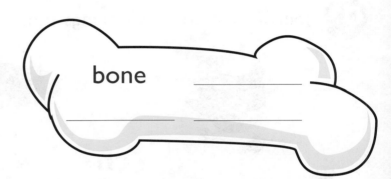

bone _____

_____   _____

Q3 Change one letter to make a new word.

race → ____ace

bake → b____ke

nose → ____ose

fire → fi____e

5

mule → m____le

mice → ____ice

Spelling patterns: sh, ch, th

Listen to **sh**, **ch** and **th** in these words.

sheep

cheese

thumb

Q1 Join **sh** and **ch** to the things that start with their sound.

ch   **sh**

What does a
sea monster eat
for lunch?

Fish and ships!

Q2 Write **sh**, **ch** or **th** at the end of each word.

fi____   bea____   pa____   bru____

ru____   mo____   fini____   lun____

Word ending: ck

Listen to the sound of **ck** at the end of clo**ck**.

The spelling pattern **ck** is only used after a short vowel.

Q1 Complete the rhymes. Choose a **ck** word to write in each space.

> sock   clock   stuck   struck

Hickory Dickory Dock,
A mouse ran up the _____.
The clock _____ one,
The mouse ran down,
Hickory Dickory Dock.

Hickory Dickory Dock,
A mouse chewed a hole in my _____.
My toe _____ out,
The mouse ran about,
Hickory Dickory Dock.

Q2 Read the **ck** words in the wall below.

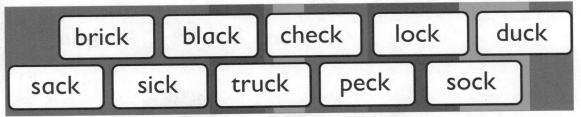

brick   black   check   lock   duck
sack   sick   truck   peck   sock

Colour the bricks. Use a different colour for each pair of rhyming words.

Word ending: ng

Listen to the sound of **ng** at the end of ri**ng**.

Q1 Lots of noisy words end in **ng**. Write **ng** at the end of each word.

ba____!

cla____!

do____!

di____!

bo____!

Q2 Cross out the wrong word.

A (strong   string) man.

Very (lung   long) hair.

A very loud (pong   song) .

Word endings: ff, ll, ss

These words all end with a **double consonant**.

gruff

well

princess

The double consonant in each word makes a single sound.

Q1 Write **ff**, **ll** or **ss** in each space.

Humpty Dumpty sat on a wa____,

Humpty Dumpty had a big fa____.

The prince____ gave the

frog a ki____.

I'll hu____ and I'll pu____ and I'll blow your

house down!

Why is Cinderella
no good at hockey?

Because she is
always running away
from the ball!

More than one

We usually add **s** to the end of a word when there is more than one of something.

one leg   lots of leg**s**

For a word that ends in **s**, **x**, **sh** or **ch**, we usually add **es**.

bus**es**   fox**es**   brush**es**   peach**es**

Q1   Add **s** or **es** to the end of each word.

a bunch of

a pair of sock____   banana____   some sweet____

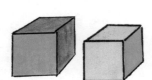

dish____   box____   monster____

sandwich____   spider____   octopus____

Colour words

Q1 Label the balloons.

red yellow pink green blue orange purple

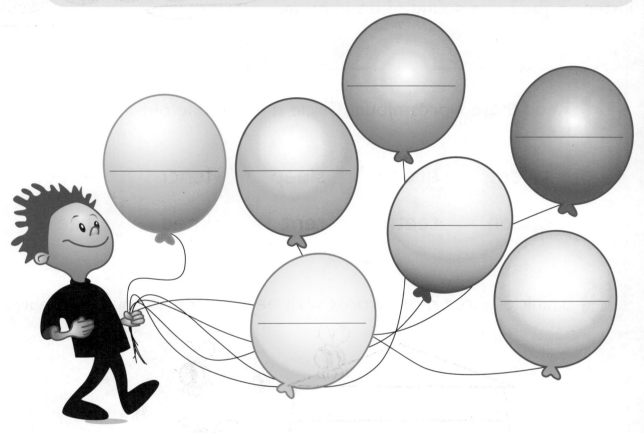

Q2 Unscramble the letters and write the colours.

wnrbo   ewith   cklab

_____   _____   _____

Vowel sound: ee, ea

Listen to the sound of **ee** in b**ee**.

Listen to the same sound of **ea** in b**ea**d.

Q1 Read these words aloud. Circle the odd one out in each row.

sweet   green   sleep   fence   street

queen   teeth   tent   knee   free

Q2 Think of three more words with **ee**. Write them on the beehive.

bee

Q3 Read these words aloud. Colour the odd one out in each row.

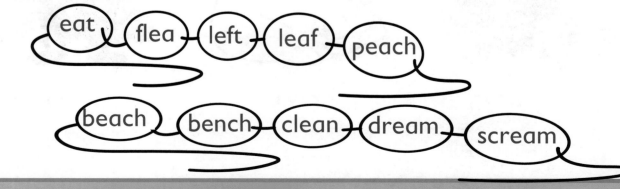

eat   flea   left   leaf   peach

beach   bench   clean   dream   scream

Vowel sound: ai, ay

Listen to the sound of **ai** in sn**ai**l.

The **ai** sound is usually spelt **ay** at the end of words.

Listen to the same sound of **ay** in pl**ay**.

Q1 Use the letters below to write words that rhyme with **snail**.

m
t
n
tr
fr

+ ail

snail

_____

_____

_____

_____

_____

Q2 Write **ai** or **ay** in these words.

tr____   tr____n   tod____

aw____   afr____d   s____

cl____   st____   p____nt

Vowel sound: ie, y, igh

Listen to the sound of **ie** in p**ie**.

Listen to the sound of **y** in fl**y**.

Listen to the same sound of **igh** in h**igh**.

Q1 Write rhyming words with **y** or **ie**.

fly   cr____   t____

fr____   p____   sp____

tr____   wh____   l____

fly

What is the difference between a bird and a fly?

A bird can fly but a fly can't bird!

Q2 Write rhyming words with **igh**.

n____ ____ ____ ____   fr____ ____ ____ ____

fl____ ____ ____ ____   br____ ____ ____ ____

l____ ____ ____ ____   m____ ____ ____ ____

r____ ____ ____ ____   s____ ____ ____ ____

knight

Q3 Finish the sentences. Write a word with **igh** in each space.

My shoes are too t____ ____ ____ ____ .

The train ride gave me a fr____ ____ ____ ____ .

16

Vowel sound: oa, ow

Listen to the sound of **oa** in b**oa**t.

Listen to the same sound of **ow** in yell**ow**.

Q1 Use these words to complete the word puzzle below.

> sparrow   coat   arrow   moat   elbow   toast   snow   coast

1 You use this to bend your arm.

2 A ditch filled with water that surrounds a castle.

3 A slice of bread heated until it turns brown.

4 A small brown bird.

5 Where the land meets the sea.

6 A pointed stick with feathers on the end.

7 White, frozen water that falls from the sky.

8 You wear this over your other clothes.

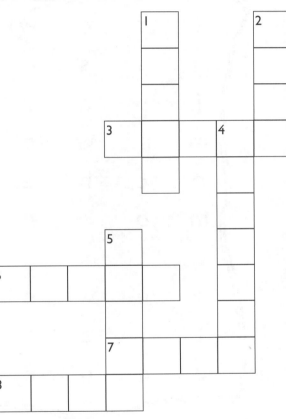

Q2 Now find three pairs of rhyming words in the word puzzle and write them in the spaces below.

1 _____   _____

2 _____   _____

3 _____   _____

Vowel sound: oo, ew, ue

Listen to the sound of **oo** in b**oo**t.

Listen to the sound of **ew** in n**ew**.

Listen to the same sound of **ue** in bl**ue**.

Q1 Circle words with **oo**, **ew** and **ue**.

i	f	e	w	x	p	i	z	o	o
y	s	s	o	o	n	c	d	w	q
j	p	h	r	e	s	c	u	e	a
m	m	w	p	b	z	g	l	u	e
o	c	h	e	w	t	t	p	l	k
m	o	o	n	g	a	r	g	u	e
q	l	x	g	l	f	l	e	w	r
j	e	w	e	l	j	s	e	m	f
t	i	s	s	u	e	p	o	h	l
a	a	y	c	o	o	l	f	m	s

Q2 Write the words you have circled in the table below.

oo	ew	ue

18

Spelling pattern: ar

Listen to the sound of **ar** in sc**ar**f.

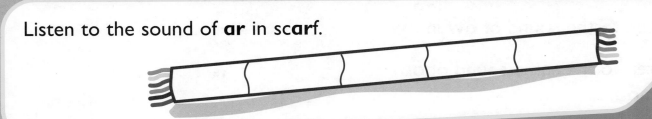

Q1 Write the letters below in the **ar** words on the scarf.

p ch m g y

far____ shar____ part____ mar____ ____arden

Q2 Use the letters below to write rhyming words inside the shark and the star.

c p j d m f

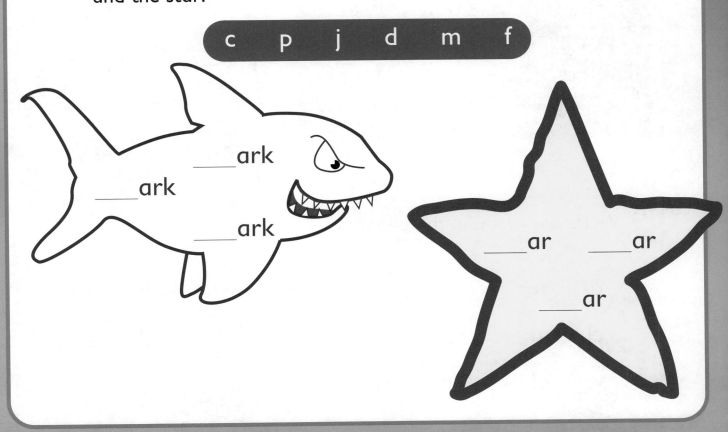

____ark

____ark

____ark

____ar   ____ar

____ar

OW, OU

Listen to the sound of **ow** in **ow**l.

Listen to the same sound of **ou** in m**ou**se.

Q1 Read the rhyme aloud. Underline ten **ow** and **ou** words.

"Watch out!" called a cat
To a mouse by a tree,
"There's an owl on the prowl.
Why not hang out with me?"

So the mouse jumped down
From his hiding place.
The cat pounced and Mouse
Disappeared without a trace.

What did the owl say to his friend as he flew away?

"Owl be seeing you later!"

Q2 Write **ow** or **ou** in these words.

d___n   f___nd   br___n   h___se

cl___n   sh___er   c___nt   fl___er

v___el   m___th   s___nd   t___n

20

air, are, ear, ere

These rhyming words all share the same sound but have a different spelling pattern.

chair **sp**are **b**ear **th**ere

Q1 Write these words in the correct column.

wear there repair tear stair scare where spare

air	are	ear	ere

Some words sound the same but are spelt differently.

Where is my hat?

I want to **wear** it to the match.

Why did the doll blush?

Because she saw the teddy bear!

Q2 Circle the correct word to label each picture.

pear pair

hair hare

stair stare

bear bare

or, oor, aw, au, ore

These words all share the same sound but have a different spelling pattern.

for   door   paw   naughty   more

Q1 Write **or** in these words.

t____ch   f___k

st____y   st____m   st___k

Q2 Say these words out loud. Circle the odd one out.

lawn   dawn   thorn

down   corn   yawn

Q3 Join up the rhyming words.

floor   crawl   sport   caught   draw

short   snore   taught   law   shawl

er, ir, ur

These words all share the same sound but have a different spelling pattern.

tig**er**

b**ir**d

t**ur**tle

Q1 Label the pictures. Then write the words in the table. Add one more of your own in each column.

sh_____

p_____

m_____

d_____

13

th_____

t_____

er	ir	ur

wh, ph, ch

Listen to the sound of **wh** in **wh**ale.

Listen to the sound of **ph** in ele**ph**ant.

Listen to the sound of **ch** in or**ch**estra.

Q1 These labels are spelt wrongly. Write the correct word.

dolfin *x* _____

weel *x* _____

quoir *x* _____

scool *x* _____

Lots of question words begin with **wh**.

who   what   when   where   why   which

Q2 Join each question to the correct answer.

1 **Wh**ere do children go to learn?   A **ch**emist

2 **Wh**ich animal is the largest   A s**ch**ool
   sea creature?

3 **Wh**y might you use a camera?   A **wh**ale

4 **Wh**at do we call the letters a   To take a **ph**oto
   to z?

5 **Wh**o might you buy   The al**ph**abet
   medicine from?

Q3 Write the meaning of each of these words.
   The first one has been done for you.

sphere   An object that is round like a ball.

graph   _____

echo   _____

ache   _____

wheat   _____

whistle _____

ear (hear), ea (head)

Listen to the sound of **ear** in h**ear**.

Q1 Use the letters below to make words that rhyme with **ear**.

y
d
n
f
sp
g
cl
r
app
t

_____   _____

_____   _____

_____   _____

_____   _____

Listen to the sound of **ea** in h**ea**vy.

Q2 Join each word to a matching picture.

head

weather

bread

breakfast

Compound words

A compound word is a word made up of two other words.

 newspaper

Q1 Join up the words to make new words.

water	cup	waterfall
tooth	house	_____
light	fall	_____
egg	day	_____
birth	brush	_____

Q2 Write the missing compound word in each joke.

> jellyfish   honeycomb   football   sunglasses

Why did the teacher wear _____?
Because her class was so bright!

Why did the _____ player wear a bib?
Because he was always dribbling!

What do _____ say at the start of a race?
Get set!

Why did the bee have sticky hair?
Because of his _____!

Prefixes: un, dis

We can add **un** and **dis** in front of some words to change their meaning and make **opposite** words.

tidy

untidy

appear

disappear

Q1 Finish writing the label under each picture.

un_____

un_____

un_____

un_____

Q2 Write **un** or **dis** in front of each word to make an opposite word.

____pack   ____agree   ____lucky   ____kind

____honest   ____fair   ____true   ____sure

Suffixes: ful, ly

We can add **ful** and **ly** to the end of some words to make describing words.

care**ful**

'shhh'

quiet**ly**

There is no word in English ending in **-full** except full!

Q1 Add **ful** or **ly** to each word.

pain____   silent____   sudden____

help____   quick____   thought____

exact____   slow____   forget____

Q2 Now choose a word to label each picture.

_____   _____

_____   _____

Spelling tips

Silly sentences can help you remember how to spell a word.

big elephants can't always use small exits → because!

gentle elephants never tackle little elephants → gentle!

Q1 Finish these silly sentences to help you remember how to spell **people** and **beauty**.

pink   big

elephants   elephants

o_____   a_____

p_____   u_____

l_____   t_____

e_____   y_____

Look for words inside words.

I like **ice** in my ju**ice**.

Q2 Underline a smaller word inside each of these words.

monkey when garage chocolate

danger brilliant cupboard comfortable

Q3 Hide each of these words inside a larger word.

put <u>**computer**</u> elf _____ pin _____

owl _____ ear _____ itch _____

Watch out for silent letters.

com**b**

Q4 Circle the silent letter inside each of these words.

thumb knee write honest

knit castle autumn knight

Answers

Short vowels
Page 4
Q1   jam, pen, bun, zip
       bed, bag, wig, dog

Q2   cat – cut, leg – log

Rhyming words
Page 5
Q1   red, fox, map

Q2   hat   sun   peg   bat   win   beg   bin
         pot   rat   tin   dot
       hot   run   leg   fun

Long vowels with e
Page 6
Q1   cube, note, kite, plane

Page 7
Q2

Happy Birthday
cake   make
rake   shake

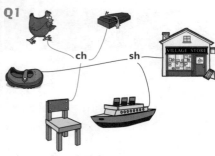

bone   cone
stone   throne

Q3   face, bike, rose, five, mole, dice

Spelling patterns: sh, ch, th
Page 8
Q1

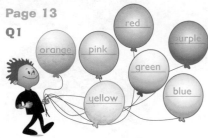

ch   sh

Q2   fish, beach, path, brush
       rush, moth, finish, lunch

Word ending: ck
Page 9
Q1   A mouse ran up the clock
       The clock struck one
       A mouse chewed a hole in my sock
       My toe stuck out

Q2   brick – sick, black – sack,
       check – peck, lock – sock,
       duck – truck

Word ending: ng
Page 10
Q1   bang, clang, dong, ding, bong

Q2   strong, long, song

Word ending: ff, ll, ss
Page 11
Q1   wall, fall
       princess, kiss
       huff, puff

More than one
Page 12
Q1   socks, bananas, sweets,
       dishes, boxes, monsters,
       sandwiches, spiders, octopuses

Colour words
Page 13
Q1

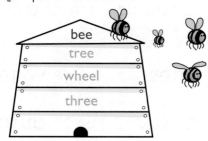

red   purple   orange   pink   green   yellow   blue

Q2   brown, white, black

Vowel sound: ee, ea
Page 14
Q1   fence, tent

Q2   possible answers are:

bee
tree
wheel
three

Q3   left, bench

Vowel sound: ai, ay
Page 15
Q1

snail
mail
tail
nail
trail
frail

Q2   tray, train, today
       away, afraid, say
       clay, stay, paint

Vowel sound: ie, y, igh
Page 16
Q1   fly, cry, tie
       fry, pie, spy
       try, why, lie

Q2   night, fright
       flight, bright
       light, might
       right, sight

Q3   tight, fright

Vowel sound: oa, ow
Page 17
Q1

Crossword:
1. elbow
2. moat
3. toast
4. sparrow
5. crow
6. arrow
7. snow
8. coat

Q2   1   moat, coat
       2   arrow, sparrow
       3   toast, coast